A year of Introits

Twenty-one settings of the Introductory Sentences in the ASB

Simon Mold, Harrison Oxley
Noel Rawsthorne & Alan Ridout

Kevin Mayhew

We hope you enjoy the music in *A Year of Introits*. Further copies are available from your local music shop or Christian bookshop.

In case of difficulty, please contact the publisher direct by writing to:

The Sales Department
KEVIN MAYHEW LTD
Rattlesden
Bury St Edmunds
Suffolk
IP30 0SZ

Phone 0449 737978
Fax 0449 737834

Please ask for our complete catalogue of outstanding Church Music.

First published in Great Britain in 1993 by Kevin Mayhew Ltd.

© Copyright 1993 Kevin Mayhew Ltd.

ISBN 0 86209 470 4

The music and texts in this book are protected by copyright and may not be reproduced in any way for sale or private use without the consent of the copyright owner.

Front Cover design by Juliette Clarke.
Picture Research: Jane Rayson.

Music setting by Kate Emerson.
Printed and bound in Great Britain.

Contents

		Page
1	Ninth Sunday before Christmas to Saturday before Advent	7
2	Advent Sunday to Christmas Eve	8
3	Christmas Day to Eve of Epiphany	10
4	Christmas Day to Eve of Epiphany	12
5	Epiphany to Epiphany 6	13
6	Epiphany to Epiphany 6	14
7	Ninth Sunday before Easter to Shrove Tuesday	17
8	Ash Wednesday to Saturday before Lent 5	18
9	Lent 5 to Wednesday in Holy Week	20
10	Easter Day to Eve of Ascension	22
11	Ascension Day to Eve of Pentecost	24
12	Pentecost	25
13	Pentecost	26
14	Trinity Sunday	29
15	After Pentecost	30
16	After Pentecost	31
17	After Pentecost	32
18	After Pentecost	34
19	Times of Thanksgiving	36
20	General	38
21	General	40

Foreword

A Year of Introits contains musical settings of twenty one Introductory Sentences, or Introits, from the *Alternative Service Book*. It will provide parish choirs with attractive material throughout the year and may be used at Morning or Evening Prayer, or at Holy Communion.

With the exception of three of the pieces, the settings are all in unison or two-parts and may be sung by mixed voices, dividing as is felt best. Harrison Oxley's composition at No. 20 may be sung either in unison (using the soprano line), by sopranos and altos only, in three parts (omitting the tenor line), or in four parts with or without organ accompaniment. The seven pieces by Alan Ridout can be performed outside of the liturgy as a cycle. They should be sung in the order they are given here with the overall title *Sacred Songs: Set 7*. They are dedicated to Patrick Wedd and the Montreal Boys' Choir.

1 NINTH SUNDAY BEFORE CHRISTMAS TO SATURDAY BEFORE ADVENT

Text : Hebrews 1:1-2   Music : Alan Ridout

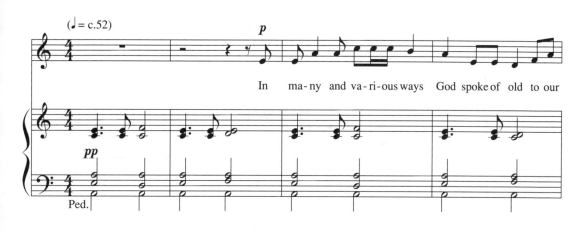
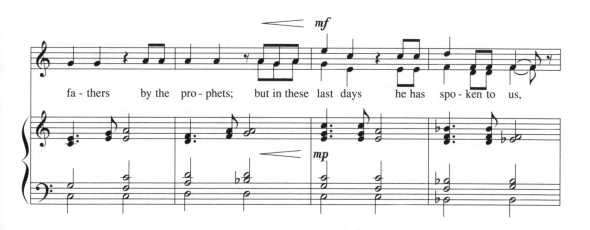
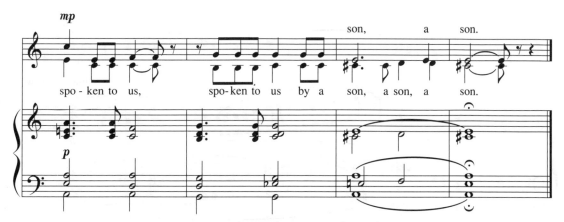

© Copyright 1993 by Kevin Mayhew Ltd.
It is illegal to photocopy music.

2 ADVENT SUNDAY TO CHRISTMAS EVE

Text : 1 Corinthians 4:5   Music : Harrison Oxley

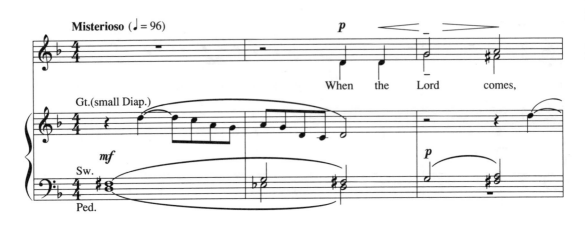

The lower voice part may be omitted

© Copyright 1993 by Kevin Mayhew Ltd.
It is illegal to photocopy music.

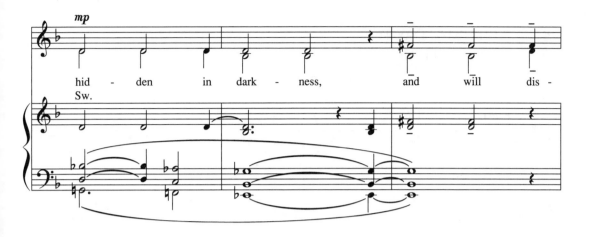

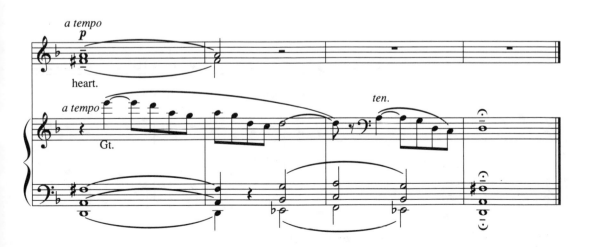

3 CHRISTMAS DAY TO EVE OF EPIPHANY

Text : Luke 2:10-11   Music : Harrison Oxley

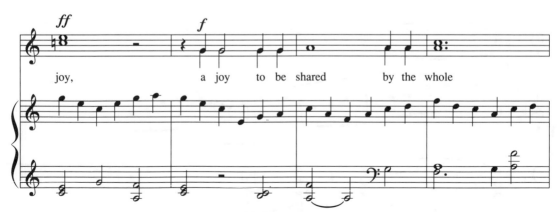

© Copyright 1993 by Kevin Mayhew Ltd.
It is illegal to photocopy music.

4 CHRISTMAS DAY TO EVE OF EPIPHANY

Text : 1 John 4:9   Music : Alan Ridout

© Copyright 1993 by Kevin Mayhew Ltd.
It is illegal to photocopy music.

5 EPIPHANY TO EPIPHANY 6

Text : Titus 2:11   Music : Alan Ridout

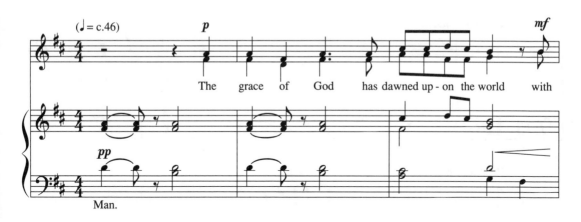

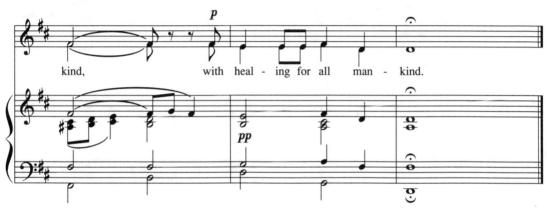

© Copyright 1993 by Kevin Mayhew Ltd.
It is illegal to photocopy music.

6 EPIPHANY TO EPIPHANY 6

Text : Malachi 1:11   Music : Simon Mold

© Copyright 1993 by Kevin Mayhew Ltd.
It is illegal to photocopy music.

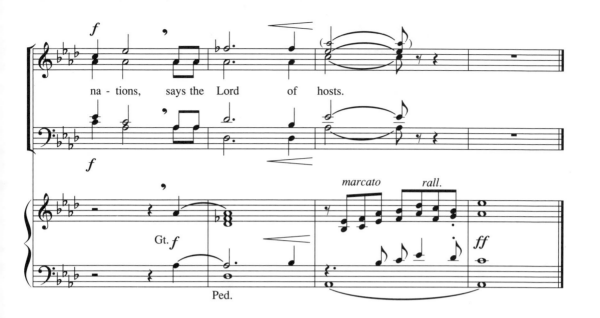

7 NINTH SUNDAY BEFORE EASTER TO SHROVE TUESDAY

Text : Matthew 11:28   Music : Noel Rawsthorne

© Copyright 1993 by Kevin Mayhew Ltd.
It is illegal to photocopy music.

8 ASH WEDNESDAY TO SATURDAY BEFORE LENT 5

Text : Daniel 9:9   Music : Alan Ridout

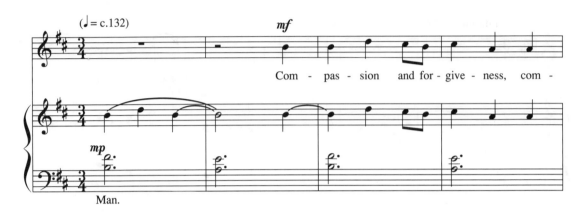

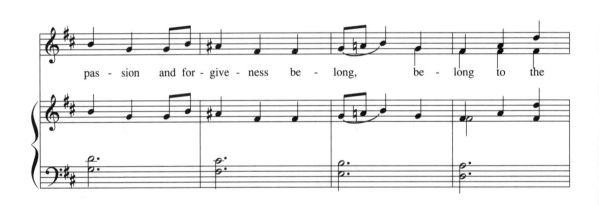

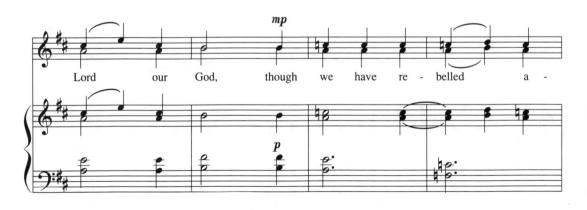

© Copyright 1993 by Kevin Mayhew Ltd.
It is illegal to photocopy music.

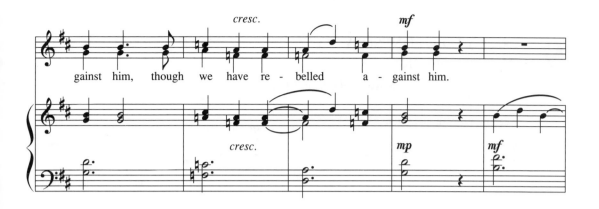
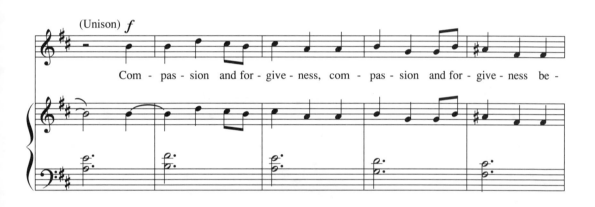

9. LENT 5 TO WEDNESDAY IN HOLY WEEK

Text: Galatians 6:14   Music: Harrison Oxley

© Copyright 1993 by Kevin Mayhew Ltd.
It is illegal to photocopy music.

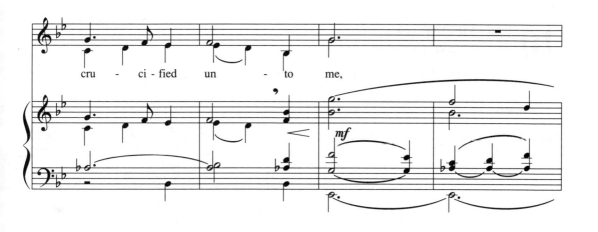
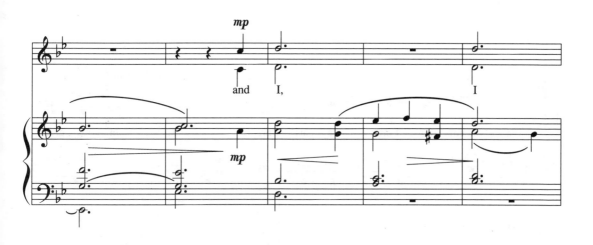
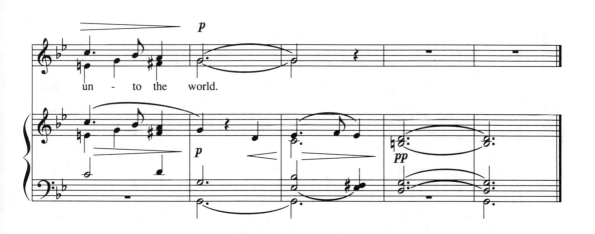

10 EASTER DAY TO EVE OF ASCENSION

Text : 1 Peter 1:3   Music : Harrison Oxley

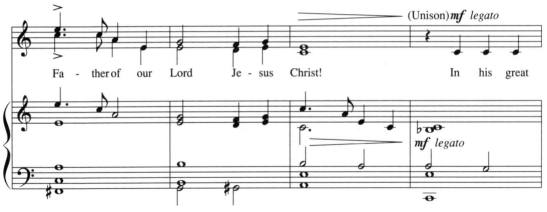

© Copyright 1993 by Kevin Mayhew Ltd.
It is illegal to photocopy music.

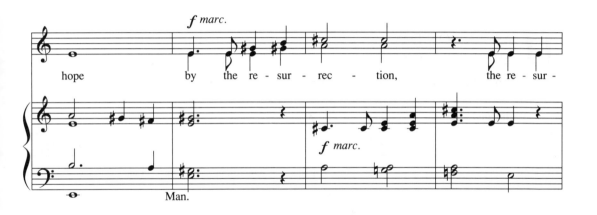

12 PENTECOST

Text : Romans 5:5 Music : Noel Rawsthorne

13 PENTECOST

Text : Acts 1:8   Music : Simon Mold

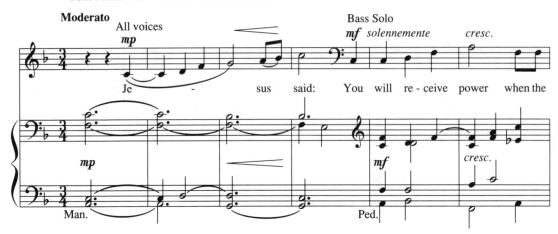

14 TRINITY SUNDAY

Text : Revelation 4:8   Music : Alan Ridout

15 AFTER PENTECOST

Text : Psalm 124:8 Music : Noel Rawsthorne

16 AFTER PENTECOST

Text : Matthew 28:20   Music : Noel Rawsthorne

© Copyright 1993 by Kevin Mayhew Ltd.
It is illegal to photocopy music.

17 AFTER PENTECOST

Text : 2 Corinthians 5:17   Music : Alan Ridout

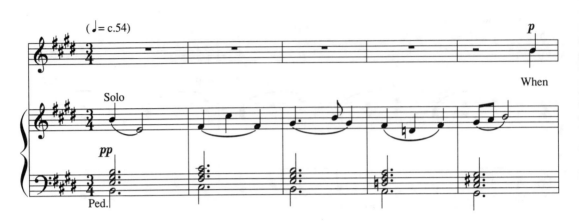
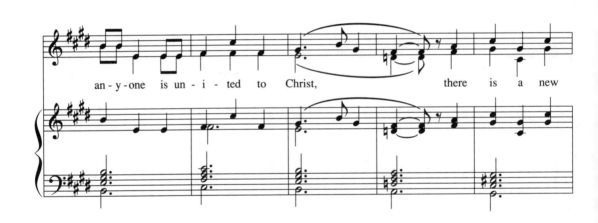

© Copyright 1993 by Kevin Mayhew Ltd.
It is illegal to photocopy music.

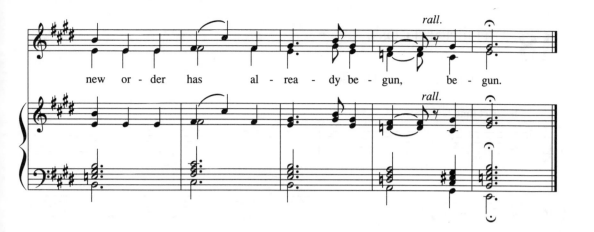

18 AFTER PENTECOST

Text : Jude:25   Music : Harrison Oxley

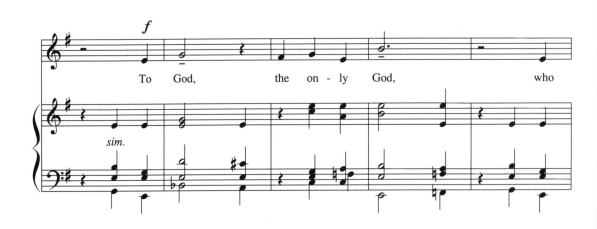
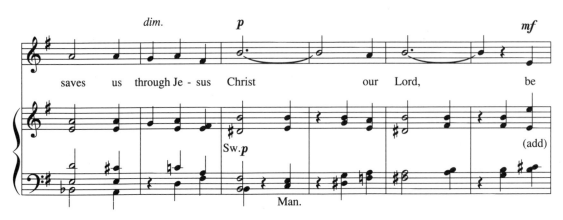

© Copyright 1993 by Kevin Mayhew Ltd.
It is illegal to photocopy music.

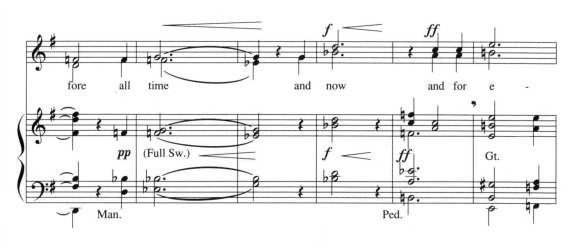
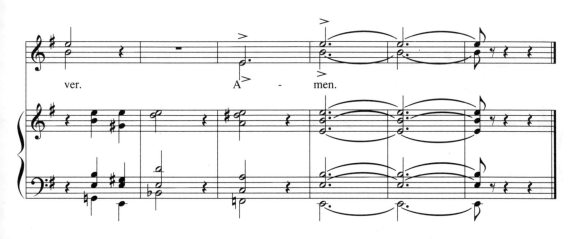

19 TIMES OF THANKSGIVING

Text : Psalm 67:4   Music : Harrison Oxley

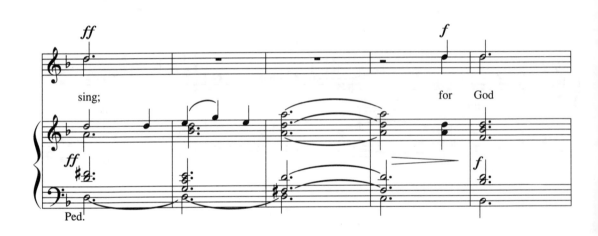
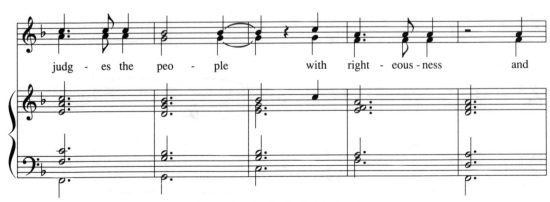

© Copyright 1993 by Kevin Mayhew Ltd.
It is illegal to photocopy music.

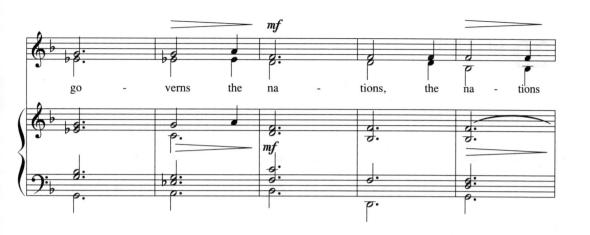
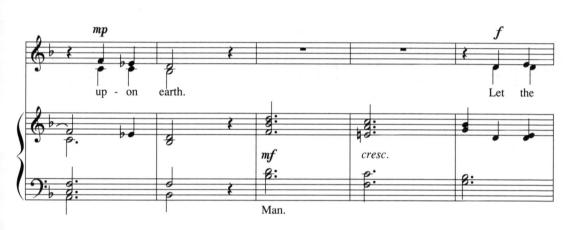
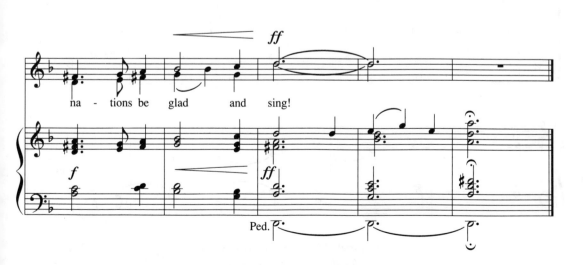

20 GENERAL

Text : Isaiah 55:6   Music : Harrison Oxley

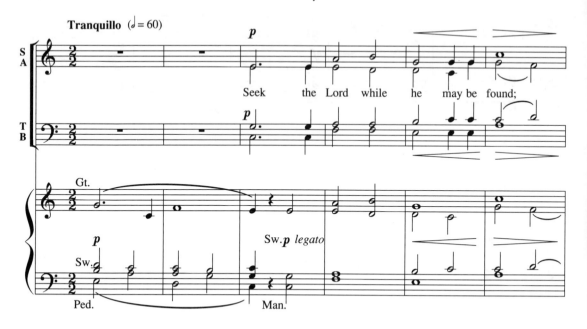
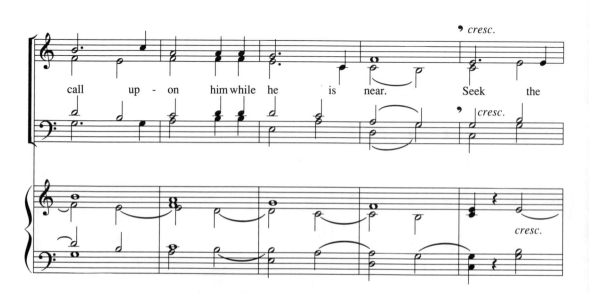

© Copyright 1993 by Kevin Mayhew Ltd.
It is illegal to photocopy music.